OUT TC

Riddles abou..

by June Swanson
pictures by Susan Slattery Burke

Lerner Publications Company
Minneapolis

To Laura and Greg for all their help —J.S.

*To my wonderful daughter, Perrin, for her inspiration in this first year
of her life —S.S.B.*

Copyright © 1994 by Lerner Publications Company

This book is available in two editions:
Library binding by Lerner Publications Company
Soft cover by First Avenue Editions
241 First Avenue North
Minneapolis, MN 55401

Library of Congress Cataloging-in-Publication Data

Swanson, June.
  Out to dry : riddles about deserts/by June Swanson ; pictures
by Susan Slattery Burke.
    p. cm. — (You must be joking!)
  ISBN 0-8225-2343-4
  1. Riddles, Juvenile. 2. Deserts—Juvenile humor. [1. Deserts—
Wit and humor. 2. Riddles. 3. Jokes.] I. Burke, Susan Slattery, ill.
II. Title. III. Series.
PN6371.S586 1994
818'.5402—dc20   93-29294
                                                         CIP
                                                          AC
Manufactured in the United States of America

1 2 3 4 5 6 – I/JR – 99 98 97 96 95 94

Q: Who was Dorothy
looking for
in the desert?

A: The Lizard of Oz.

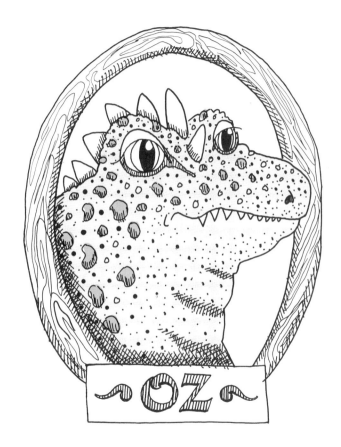

Q: Why did the roadrunner lay an egg in the middle of the road?

A: She wanted to lay it on the line.

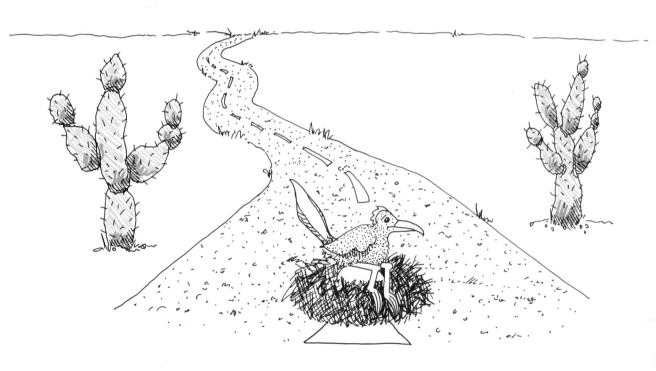

Q: Why did the football team go to the desert?
A: To warm up before the game.

Q: Why was it so hot at the desert football game?
A: There weren't any fans there.

Q: Why did the archaeologist leave the desert?
A: Her job was in ruins.

Q: What did the roadrunner think about the Grand Canyon?
A: It was just gorges.

Q: Where's the desert cemetery?
A: In Death Valley.

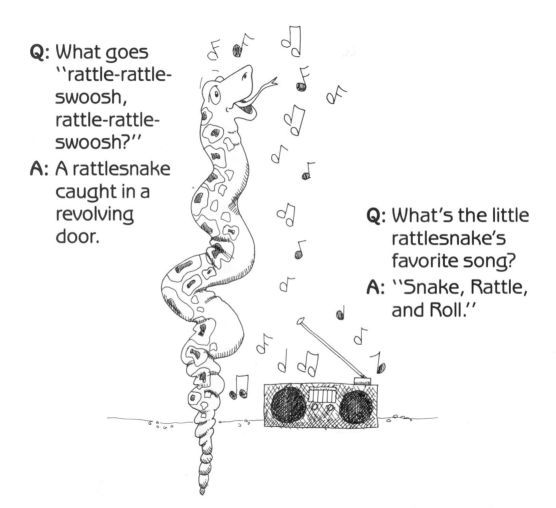

Q: What goes "rattle-rattle-swoosh, rattle-rattle-swoosh?"

A: A rattlesnake caught in a revolving door.

Q: What's the little rattlesnake's favorite song?

A: "Snake, Rattle, and Roll."

Q: What did the cactus do to get everyone out of its way?

A: It blew its thorns.

Q: What did the cactus call its trip to the barbershop?

A: A needleless experience.

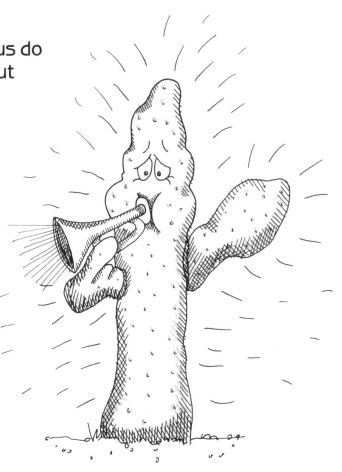

Q: What's the little cactus's favorite song?
A: "Dune in the Valley."

Q: What's the little cactus's favorite nursery rhyme?
A: "Needle, Needle Dumpling."

Q: How do you think the fight between Huck the coyote and Finn the jackrabbit will turn out?
A: Huck'll bury Finn.

Q: Why did the dog follow the cat across the desert?
A: He was in hot purr-suit.

Q: What did the coyote say when she heard the jackrabbit was leaving the desert?
A: "Oh, well—hare today, gone tomorrow."

Q: What two cactuses did Alice meet in Wonderland?
A: Needledee and Needledum.

Q: What did she call them?
A: A prickly pear.

Q: What did the cat say when he bumped into the cactus?

A: "Me-ouch!"

Q: How did the little camel describe her trip across the desert?

A: "Easier said than dune."

Q: What did the prairie dog ask the sunburned banana?
A: ''How're you peeling?''

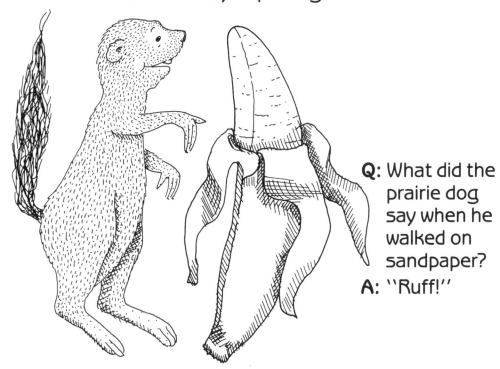

Q: What did the prairie dog say when he walked on sandpaper?
A: ''Ruff!''

Q: What did the cactus say to the bank teller?
A: "I needle little money."

Q: What does a desert doctor always carry?
A: A thirst aid kit.

Q: How did the doctor take the little cactus's temperature?
A: With a thornometer.

Q: Where do you save your water in the desert?
A: In the Thirst National Bank.

Q: What would you call a cheerful jackrabbit?

A: A happy hoppy.

Q: What do you have when the desert sun shines down a jackrabbit hole?

A: Hot, cross bunnies.

Q: What did the hiker say when she stepped on the cactus?

A: ''Yucca!''

Q: What do you get if you cross a gymnast and a dandelion?

A: A tumbleweed.

Q: What do you call fudge made in the desert?
A: Sandy candy.

Q: Who puts baby camels to bed?
A: The sandman.

Q: What's round, lives in the desert, and bites people?
A: A mesquite-o.

Q: What's brown, cold and creamy, and rattles?
A: A chocolate milksnake.

Q: What famous ancestor of the rattlesnake wrote plays?
A: William Snakespeare.

Q: Where does the wise old desert owl live?
A: In the sagebrush.

Q: How can you tell when a cactus has a magnetic personality?
A: Its needles point north.

Q: Why did the cactus call the dune a sissy?
A: The dune wouldn't sand up to him.

Q: In what month was the little sandstorm born?
A: Au-gust.

Q: Why did the baby snake cry?
A: She lost her rattle.

Q: What new hobby did the cactus take up?
A: Needlepoint.

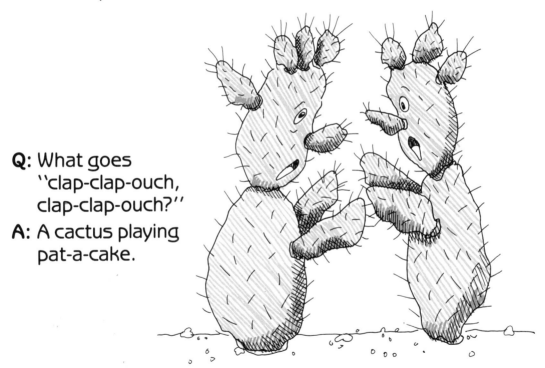

Q: What goes
"clap-clap-ouch,
clap-clap-ouch?"
A: A cactus playing
pat-a-cake.

Q: Why is everyone on the Gobi Desert friendly?
A: Because there are no-mads there.

Q: How did the nomads hide on the desert?
A: They used camel-flage.

Q: What did the artist use to draw a mirage?
A: Disappearing ink.

Q: Did you hear the news about the blowing sand?
A: It's all over the desert.

Q: What do you get if you cross the Mojave Desert with a grandfather clock?

A: The sands of time.

Q: What did the desert card player say when he picked up his hand?
A: "O-asis!"

Q: What did the little mirage do for the desert talent show?
A: A disappearing act.

Q: How did the magician describe a mirage?
A: "Now you see it, now you don't!"

Q: Why did the gambler go to the desert?
A: He was looking for a hot tip.

Q: What has 100 candles on its birthday cake?
A: A century plant.

Q: How many hairs are in a coyote's tail?
A: None. They're all on the outside.

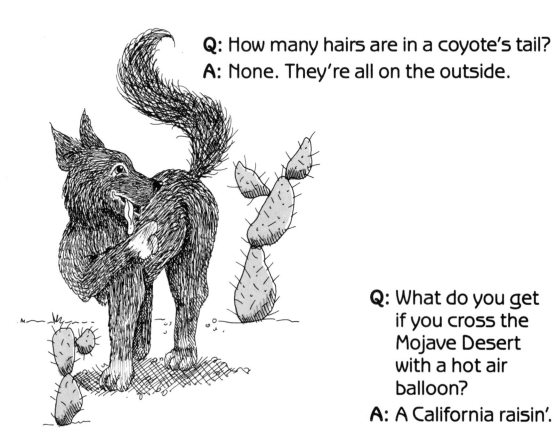

Q: What do you get if you cross the Mojave Desert with a hot air balloon?
A: A California raisin'.

Q: What would a farmer have if a cactus grew in his hayfield?

A: Needles in a haystack.

Q: What do you call it when camels run from one waterhole to the next?

A: Oases races.

Q: Did you hear the story about the bare cactus?

A: It was pointless.

Q: What happened when the coyote left his fishing worms in the desert sun?

A: He heated debate.

Q: What did the roadrunner do every morning before she ran?

A: Her worm-up exercises.

Q: What happened when the roadrunner stuck his head in the toaster?

A: He got an electric bill.

Q: Then what did the coyote ask the roadrunner?

A: "Sahara you feeling?"

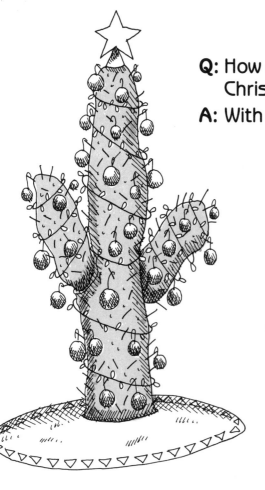

Q: How do you decorate a cactus for Christmas?

A: With thornaments.

Q: Why did Rudolph go to the desert?

A: He was looking for the Santa Fe trail.

Q: What was the tumbleweed's New Year's resolution?

A: To turn over a new leaf.

Q: What would you call a tired tarantula?
A: A sleepy creepy.

Q: What would you call a scorpion with a southern accent?
A: A drawly crawly.

Q: How can you tell if a gila monster likes you?
A: He'll take another bite.

ABOUT THE AUTHOR

June Swanson began her career by writing magazine articles and short stories. After having almost 200 published—for both children and adults—she turned to writing books. This is her fifth published book. June is a graduate of the University of Texas, and she has a master's degree in English from Florida Atlantic University. She lives in New Hampshire and enjoys hiking, skiing, collecting antiques, and visiting her four children and nine grandchildren.

ABOUT THE ARTIST

Susan Slattery Burke loves to illustrate fun-loving characters, especially animals. To her, each of her characters has a personality all its own. She is most satisfied when the characters come to life for the reader as well. Susan lives in Minnetonka, Minnesota, with her husband, two daughters, and their dog and cat. Susan enjoys sculpting, reading, traveling, illustrating, and chasing her children around.

You Must Be Joking books

Alphabatty
Riddles from A to Z

Help Wanted
Riddles about Jobs

Here's to Ewe
Riddles about Sheep

Hide and Shriek
Riddles about Ghosts and Goblins

Ho Ho Ho!
Riddles about Santa Claus

Home on the Range
Ranch-Style Riddles

Hoop-La
Riddles about Basketball

I Toad You So
Riddles about Frogs and Toads

Off Base
Riddles about Baseball

On with the Show
Show Me Riddles

Out on a Limb
Riddles about Trees and Plants

Out to Dry
Riddles about Deserts

Summit Up
Riddles about Mountains

Take a Hike
Riddles about Football

That's for Shore
Riddles from the Beach

Weather or Not
Riddles for Rain and Shine

What's Gnu?
Riddles from the Zoo

Wing It!
Riddles about Birds